The Offer

**Following God's Pathway
For Your Life**

By

Marcy Cage

The Offer

Following God's Pathway For Your Life

Introduction

Decisions, Decisions.....

What to wear, what to cook, should I text or call, should I have that dreadful conversation, do I feel like going into work....SO MANY DECISIONS but, I must make a choice. But the biggest question that brings all my decisions to a halt is what will they think of me and will this be accepted by others. So much to consider, but I've discovered the struggle is not so much making the decision but it's choosing the right decision in comparison to what others may choose.

There are many offers a person encounters in their lifetime and when accepted they are never without consequence whether good or bad. I have found that these offers are methods (or shall I say steppingstone) in which a person takes with the intention of a greater gain. For instance, after going on a job interview the next step one expects is to receive a job offer. The acceptance or declination of this job offer is dependent upon how this offer aligns and/or helps the individual reach their intended goal. It seems that no one wants to accept anything that sends them away from their goals no matter how great it may seem but sometimes when we find ourselves in an impossible situation this may not be the case. This book is not about the general definition of what the offer is. It is about the "ultimate offer", that keeps one holding on, not only when they are in an impossible situation but also when they have been inspired with dreams, goals and ideas that only God himself can give. This book encourages and inspires you to look ahead even when the past seems to look more pleasant. It is through following God that we able to have a secured victory no matter what challenges we face along the way. I encourage you to journey with me in discovering the "ultimate" offer.

Dreams, Goals, and Ideas

As a young child, I always had dreams about doing something great; as I got older these dreams became more defined and I was able to write them out and set goals accordingly. Throughout time, challenges arose bringing discomfort, fear, anxiety and ultimately delay as it relates to both my goals and desires. In addition to this, I have been in prayer about things in which God has given me His word about and have challenged myself to fully trust and depend on Him. As time moved on the desire to accomplish the goals grew a bit intimidating and stressful, at times. The most common attribute individuals have is their need to be validated or have approval. It seems that we have been molded with this attribute from infancy. As soon as we begin to speak our first few words, we subconsciously are conditioned that the better we do then the more praise we get from those around us. This concept follows us to adulthood and for many individuals it remains with them throughout their entire lives, it is known as the need to please everyone. Validation puts us in a direction of life by aiding us in the manner in which we will approach the things in which we set out to accomplish and depending who and what serves as our validation determines how we will carry out our purpose in life. Relationships with others is at the top of the list for things that bring us validation and has an influence on how we decide things in life. It seems that if we are going in one direction and everyone else is going in the opposite direction, we will begin to question our direction and/or choose to fall in with the rest. We cannot get so wrapped up in the need and desire to please or be accepted by others: God has to be our validation and the only one that we are set on making sure we have pleased. Otherwise, all our accomplishments will be in vain. As I reflect on my college years, I recall engaging in certain activities as a freshman not indulging in any sinful acts but putting myself in a compromising position to feel like I played my role. I recall going out to a bar one night with my new friends from the dorm. I knew that I should not have gone but decided to go anyway just to hang out with the girls. I did not drink nor dance, I literally stood on a wall and just watched those around me. Within moments of being there, I begin to feel uncomfortable and I begin to question my life as well as my Christianity. I thought about what explanation would I give to God if He were to come back in that moment or if I had died suddenly. Yes, instead of having an enjoyable time I was very miserable. That night I realized that by choosing the way in which they were going as a means of establishing relationships caused me to compromise the purpose in which God had me in this place from the very beginning. Please do not misunderstand me, God is not opposed to us having relationships with others. He wants us to remain in the direction He has for us. Perhaps, you have not been faced with this exact situation maybe you are in a position in which you are welcoming relationships in your life that do not necessarily bring you immediate harm. In fact, these relationships probably bring you comfort and confidence in who you are currently. However, you are not seeing any spiritual progression. Either way, you should not try to stay there either but instead seek God's face for the strategic relationships and for the Holy Ghost to comfort you and give you the confidence you need in life. We must conclude even if the offer is relationships, we must follow His leading so that in the end His purpose and agenda will be fulfilled.

Standing
When It Seems Like You Are
Alone

As we mature in relationship with God, He pushes us from the learned behavior of validation through others by forcing us to do and work diligently in the absence of an earthly audience and approvals. In this process, we begin learning that as long as the Holy Ghost reaffirms, we are okay to keep moving into the direction that God has set for us and He will bless us as we continue to follow His path. Let's look at Mary the mother of Jesus. When Mary became pregnant with Jesus, we can all imagine that this was an awkward time in Mary's life. She had remained pure and lived honorable before God, so the news of pregnancy was definitely "NEWS" to her. We learned that Mary in this time of her life was not immediately comforted by those around her. After all, Joseph had plans to separate from her because of this new information. It was the angel of the Lord who came to speak to Mary in this time. The gospel of Luke, Chapter 1:28-35 tells us *"And the angel came in unto her, and said, Hail, [thou that art] highly favoured, the Lord [is] with thee: blessed [art] thou among women. 29 And when she saw [him], she was troubled at his saying, and cast in her mind what manner of salutation this should be. 30 And the angel said unto her, Fear not, Mary: for thou hast found favour with God. 31 And, behold, thou shalt conceive in thy womb, and bring forth a son, and shalt call his name JESUS. 32 He shall be great, and shall be called the Son of the Highest: and the Lord God shall give unto him the throne of his father David: 33 And he shall reign over the house of Jacob for ever; and of his kingdom there shall be no end. 34 Then said Mary unto the angel, How shall this be, seeing I know not a man? 35 And the angel answered and said unto her, The Holy Ghost shall come upon thee, and the power of the Highest shall overshadow thee: therefore also that holy thing which shall be born of thee shall be called the Son of God.* " God has no plans to forsake nor leave us lonely, but He has gone ahead of us and prepared the ways for us to do what it is He is requiring of us. As we see here with Mary, it was God's plan for her to give birth to His son, but He was also there to provide her with the instructions by which she would be able to do so. Here in this moment, Mary realizes that she doesn't need others to make her feel accepted, but she can rejoice in the fact that she has favor with God and He will ensure that she is taken care of as long as she follows His directions. After this, God put Mary on the path towards a "strategic relationship" that would serve as encouragement to her as she continued the path in which God set for her. God has no plans to forsake nor leave us lonely, but He is always ahead of us preparing ways for us to do what it is He is requiring of us. Luke 1:36-45 tells us *36" And, behold, thy cousin Elisabeth, she hath also conceived a son in her old age: and this is the sixth month with her, who was called barren. 37 For with God nothing shall be impossible. 38 And Mary said, Behold the handmaid of the Lord; be it unto me according to thy word. And the angel departed from her.*

39 And Mary arose in those days, and went into the hill country with haste, into a city of Juda; 40 And entered into the house of Zacharias, and saluted Elisabeth. 41 And it came to pass, that, when Elisabeth heard the salutation of Mary, the babe leaped in her womb; *and Elisabeth was filled with the Holy Ghost: 42 And she spake out with a loud voice, and said, Blessed [art] thou among women, and blessed [is] the fruit of thy womb. 43 And whence [is] this to me, that the mother of my Lord should come to me? 44 For, lo, as soon as the voice of thy salutation sounded in mine ears, the babe leaped in my womb for joy. 45 And*
0blessed [is] she that believed: for there shall be a performance of those things which were told her from the Lord."

Both Mary and Elisabeth had a destiny to fulfill through the promises that were made to them. So, whether we admit it or not it is very difficult to be in a position in where those around you are not accepting of your decision to follow the plan of God. Especially if the individuals have been in your life for a very long time. However, neither of these women put themselves in compromising positions. Instead they focused on the spoken word, the promise and followed the instructions of the Lord versus the way in which they may have felt in that moment. In doing so, Mary looked for Elisabeth; they identified with each other. Their purposes identified with each other. They were able to build each other up as God had ordained and purposed. In life we must realize that not everyone will go along with the direction that God has for us nor will everyone be able to encourage you on that journey. It is important to know that God will place not only himself with you but there will be others on your path to encourage you to fulfill the destiny and follow the plan God has for your life. As Elisabeth said to Mary, "the babe leaped in my womb for joy". When you are connected with those individuals God has purposed for your life the Spirit of God inside of you will leap and rejoice because light has connected with light. In this as well as the Word of God, you will find the courage to stand but this time never feeling like you are alone. As it is written in 1 John 4:4 *"Ye are of*

God, little children, and have overcome them: because greater is he that is in you, than he that is in the world."

Break Out Plan B

You never achieve anything without first establishing a plan as to how you will get it done. Seemingly, there is nothing wrong with making a plan or setting goals. In reality, it is a wise thing to do right. Plans prove how serious you are about accomplishing your goals. The danger in planning comes when we neglect to go with God. When we become so a fixated with our plan, we do not allow God's freedom to steer us in His direction to achieve the plan. Every young girl and woman think of the day she will marry and start a family. The who, the what, when and the where; many plans from start to finish. As a matter of fact, most women I know have a Pinterest board titled one day, wedding day, the future Mrs. and etc., all filled with inspirations of how THE BIG DAY should actually be and from there they plan their moving into homes and having children. Perhaps guys even have some similar concepts in a secret compartment of their brain. This is not an uncommon action. It seems that we, as creatures of habit typically have some concept of the very thing we want in life and our plans to get there. So, what happens...instead of us allowing our will and desires to be confirmed to what our Heavenly Father wants, we pray and hope that He will conform to what we want. We even go as far as giving Him some assistance especially when things become really tight for us. Let's take a look at Sarai, she married Abram and had not been able to conceive, but yet her husband was promised to have many descendants. Genesis 15:4-54 says *"And, behold, the word of the Lord came to him, saying, This shall not be thine heir, but he that shall come forth out of thine own bowels shall be thine heir. Brought forth abroad, and said, Look now toward heaven, and tell the stars, if thou be able to number them: and he said unto him, So shall thy seed be."* Then, Genesis 16:1-2 says *"Now Sarai, Abram's wife, had borne him no children. But she had an Egyptian slave named Hagar; 2 so she said to Abram, "The Lord has kept me from having children. Go, sleep with my slave; perhaps I can build a family through her.*" Sarai had yielded to the influence of her vain imagination. She did not seek to understand the will of God for her and Abram's life. Her desire was that she would have a family and she had to find some way to make it happen. This is just like us, in our lives we become influenced due to our vain imaginations, because we do not make an effort to seek God in prayer until He delivers us from our own thoughts. Our minds run away with endless possibilities of how we can ensure that things will work out. In these moments we fail horribly in realizing that the God we serve is more than capable of seeing to it that we are well taken care of. As the story goes on, we learned that it was after Hagar became pregnant that God spoke to Abram. Now, Abraham regarding having a child with Sarai now Sarah. Genesis 17:15-22 tells us (15)"*God also said to Abraham, As for Sarai your wife, you are no longer to call her Sarai; her name will be Sarah. 16 I will bless her and will surely give you a son by her. I will bless her so that she will be the mother of nations; kings of peoples will come from her.17 Abraham fell facedown; he laughed and said to himself, Will a son be born to a man a hundred years old? Will Sarah bear a child at the age of ninety? 18 And Abraham said to God, If only Ishmael might live under your blessing!19 Then God said, Yes, but your wife Sarah will bear you a son, and you will call him Isaac.[d] I will establish my covenant with him as an everlasting covenant for his descendants after him. 20 And as for Ishmael, I have heard you: I will surely bless him; I will make him fruitful and will greatly increase his numbers. He will be the father of twelve rulers, and I will make him into a great nation. 21 But my covenant I will establish with Isaac, whom Sarah will bear to you by this time next year. 22 When he had finished speaking with Abraham, God went up from him."*

It is God's plan that will cause us to stand out not our own methods or ideas. God's plans regarding Abraham & Sarah had never changed. In other words, the very thing He promised would come forth through them and will never become void, it was strategically planned by God. The ideas, goals, and promises God has given us all has a strategic approach orchestrated by God. No matter the length of time it still will be fulfilled if we prayerfully follow Him. I am aware that the desire to see it happen ignites a desperation within us that leads us to our own methodology rather than prayer. Never forget that the constant conversation with God is the only way to ensure that you are following His plan.

Pressure

One of the most common issues in the human nature is our inability to wait patiently. Modern times have conditioned us that the phrase "good things come to those who wait" has a specific time limit as to how long we should wait before we classify whatever we have received is now ours because we have waited. Even children lack the ability to wait. When they are hungry, they expect to be fed immediately and when they have a need it must be met immediately, otherwise we will hear their displeasure. Therefore, from birth we have the inability to wait patiently. It is through life's journey that we develop some level of patience, but the issue lies in our ability to be fully tolerant of the process, of waiting when the moment presents itself. Once we develop a system to help us to do things more expeditiously, then our level of patience pretty much dwindles down. For example, I have always had an issue with doing laundry, I feel like the process is too long. You know the washing for 45 - 90 minutes depending on the load. Next the drying process, which will sometimes take nearly 2 additional hours. Finally, the folding, sorting, and hanging process adds another hour. Sometimes if you have multiple loads and fail to coordinate the process precisely, then laundry takes your entire day. Yes, yes, I am very impatient in this matter. Often, I am in search of ways and resources to eliminate this entire process from my life. I would much rather just wear the clothes and be done. So, what will happen if someone walks up to me today and offers to do my laundry for the rest of my life? I will accept it no questions asked because it provides me a solution for one of the most pressing issues in my life. It is exactly what I need. For many of us of that is how we live our lives daily in respect to our destiny and purpose God has for us. We are hopelessly tolerating the wait of His word coming to pass in our life but internally we have already decided if we get an offer that brings us to the fulfillment of our destiny quicker than we will take it no questions asked. In John 11:21, Martha spoke to Jesus and said *"Lord, if you had been here, my brother would not have died."* Shortly afterwards Mary says the same thing to Him. These ladies shared the understanding that the current state of their brother deemed it too late for him to recover. Lazurus was now buried, this burial was not a fresh burial, but it had been a few days since he had been buried. Perhaps, Mary and Martha had been praying when Lazarus became sick or maybe they assumed he wouldn't die because of the relationship they all had with Jesus. Either way, their response to Jesus shown that these ladies had given up hope that anything would happen for Lazarus and for them. This fragment of story speaks volumes to many of us regarding past and present situations of our life. How often have we anticipated, believed, and waited for God to answer us or bring some sort of change to our current situation? In some cases, we've even tried hard to believe Him after the time of change had passed. These moments leave us in a state of hopelessness because we not only have to battle within ourselves, but we also have to battle with the words of condemnation being spoken to us by family and friends who see that nothing has happened for us. It is the hardest thing in the world! Thankfully, we still have Jesus, just as Mary and Martha did. Let's reflect back on the text in John 11:4 "When Jesus heard that, he said, this sickness is not unto death, but for the glory of God, that the Son of God might be glorified thereby." The scripture reminds us that God had a plan and His plan was in no ways hidden from His son Jesus. It would be a matter of time before it would be revealed. God does not need us to remind Him of how long it has been since He had made a promise to us nor does He need us to forget His capabilities. His desire is that we as his children stand firm no matter what happens and not be persuaded to accept an easy fix just because the pressure of time is upon us or the feeling that opportunity has since passed us. His ultimate plan is that He would be glorified not according to man's standards but according to the word in which He has spoken concerning our lives.

Through the story of Lazarus we see that there is always a rotation for us to accept defeat especially when the pressure is very heavy or a certain point in time has passed. For instance, let's create a pressure calendar: Day 1-5: We pray and seek for an answer or help in a speak situation in our life. Day 6-7: We receive an answer or some sort of confirmation that help is on the way. Day 8: We are challenged by the enemy that we've heard wrong or perhaps we didn't even hear God's voice. Day 9: We pray again for clarity and assurance after all we must ensure that we are waiting on the right thing or doing the right thing. Day 10: We question ourselves on rather we are doing the right thing. Day 11: We are presented with different ways to get our petition before God resolved sooner. Perhaps this happened to you on day one! Day 12: We pray again but this TIME we are SURE that we are doing the right thing. Day 13-21: We continue in such confidence that all is well, and that God has worked things out for us. Day 22: We are closer to our day of expectation, so we find ourselves a bit anxious. Day 23: Activate Plan B because we are unsure if things will work out as God has promised they would. Day 24: We've taken joy in the fact that we have received what we needed to happen has happened. Day 30: We realized that what we thought was our solution was just a false idea presented by the enemy to throw us off course. This calendar may not be completely applicable to your life, because your wait time is shorter, maybe you've had patience for much longer than a few days, or you have succeeded from time to time. Either way we look at this calendar it provides us with some truth into the moments in which we spend in our lives deciding whether on 3 options:

1. Keep Following God

2. Create & Follow another plan

3. Give up.

Oftentimes, we choose one of the last two options simply because of us spending all 30 days in prayer. We begin to entertain thoughts and make agreements with the enemy contrary to what God's word has spoken to us. I found out that if we spend more days, hours, minutes, and seconds thinking and analyzing the course of our lives than we do in prayer we are less likely to keep following God. Therefore, in order to keep the determination of following God, we must remain steadfast in prayer. Even when it seems like things are taking too long in everyone's eyes are on you resist the pressure to accept another path. It may get you there quicker, but at what cost? God has a path for you to follow, remember with the idea of His glory being revealed in you.

Tired??
Don't Turn Around

Remember Lot's wife. "Whosoever shall seek to save his life shall lose it; and whosoever shall lose his life shall preserve it." I tell you, in Luke 17:32 In the previous chapter we discussed waiting and in addition I spoke on the importance of remembering. However, I do not want to neglect the fact the sometimes in life we remember the "good" things and times we had on the other side. You know the time in life when we weren't so dedicated to God. And in some cases, the decisions or things we became involved in contrary to God's will that seemed to really work out for our benefit. Perhaps, we are in a situation in which God has called us out of a particular place to begin another work for Him and we think of the times when life was much simpler for us. On this journey of life, things can become overly complicated and all your efforts to achieve and go forward will appear to be ineffective in these moments the enemy will cause you to reflect on the past, the journey before this one and its simplicity. In these times, you will begin to desire to go backwards sort of like the children of Israel. Exodus 16:3 tells us *And the children of Israel said unto them, Would to God we had died by the hand of the Lord in the land of Egypt, when we sat by the flesh pots, and when we did eat bread to the full; for ye have brought us forth into this wilderness, to kill this whole assembly with hunger."* The children of Israel begin to regret their freedom just moments after God had delivered them out of the hands of Pharaoh. Their focus seemed to have shifted to the days behind them and at this point they in some way neglected the many great acts God had performed before their very eyes. I suppose they were a bit tired and life on the other side provided them with a sense of comfort that at least there would be no surprise, no constant fight to maintain freedom.

Maybe you have been here feeling this same way thinking that there is more comfort or that it's better on the other side or better in the life you have once before compared to now. However, we must take a closer look and recognize that this is the plot of the enemy to subvert us in our course. Let's consider a few things regarding the children of Israel. The children of Israel were never supposed to be slaves because they were born a great nation. However, they adopted to the lifestyle of being held captive and settled for that which they had at the current time. So, imagine their surprise when someone comes to and tells them they can be free. It is a bit hard for them to comprehend because they only knew the life of captivity. Consider yourself and the destiny God has for you, it's something that is foreign to you. You are aware that it exists on some level but at the same time you are comfortable in the life you have and/or the position you have because it brings you comfort without battle. You must understand that there is no comfort in staying where you do not belong no matter what it feels like or looks like in this moment. By choosing not to fight, you choose to accept whatever plans the enemy has for you, missing each opportunity that God has for you. Trust me, the place in which you have left is empty, but I am sure that when the enemy presents it to you it doesn't seem that way. It looks appealing, far better than where you are now, full of opportunity and advancement but in reality, it is quite the opposite. Instead it is gloomy, lifeless, full of stagnation and dead things nothing in which you would want to go back to if you really thought about it. I entered into a phase in my life in which it seemed as if I was not accomplishing anything. Every door had been blocked and there was literally nothing for me to do or say. I worked a lot trying to find out the reason why my life was in such a way. I worked hard in ministry and did whatever God told me to do but every evening I still felt like a failure because the things in which God told me would happen in my life just weren't happening and I could not understand. So, as days passed, I begin to say I should return to this place or another because I was valued there. After much prayer and asking God to enlighten me I realize that these confessions and thoughts were just a way for the enemy to get me to miss out on what God has for me. Realizing that turning around was not worth it I gathered myself together with great determination to finish the journey.

Jesus after He had completed his forty days of fasting the scripture tells us that "*Then was Jesus led up of the Spirit into the wilderness to be tempted of the devil. ²And when he had fasted forty days and forty nights, he was afterward an hungred.³And when the tempter came to him, he said, If thou be the Son of God, command that these stones be made bread.*

⁴*But he answered and said, It is written, Man shall not live by bread alone, but by every word that proceedeth out of the mouth of God.⁵Then the devil taketh him up into the holy city, and setteth him on a pinnacle of the temple, ⁶And saith unto him, If thou be the Son of God, cast thyself down: for it is written, He shall give his angels charge concerning thee: and in their hands they shall bear thee up, lest at any time thou dash thy foot against a stone.⁷Jesus said unto him, It is written again, Thou shalt not tempt the Lord thy God.⁸Again, the devil taketh him up into an exceeding high mountain, and sheweth him all the kingdoms of the world, and the glory*

of them;⁹And saith unto him, All these things will I give thee, if thou wilt fall down and worship me.¹⁰Then saith Jesus unto him, Get thee hence, Satan: for it is written, Thou shalt worship the Lord thy God, and him only shalt thou serve.¹¹Then the devil leaveth him, and, behold, angels came and ministered unto him." I would like to believe that even though his flesh was weak His spirit man was very strong. However, Satan still desired to appeal to His flesh speaking to the fact that He was the son of man with abilities to produce food and save Himself from death if He threw himself off a cliff. He offered him things that weren't necessarily "bad" things to do but He still had to reject them because they were not the purpose and intent for His life at this time. Therefore, any attention or acceptance He put into taking part in these actions would have caused him to forfeit his destiny and not bring forth victory. So, He had to counteract the things being spoken so that He can continue in his freedom towards the fulfillment of his destiny. This is similar to our lives today; you and I must not entertain the thoughts and attempts of the enemy but reject them and declare God's word. You must shift your eyes to the things of the kingdom which will require you to see through your spiritual eyes.

It's Worth the Journey

"Wait on the Lord: be of good courage, and he shall

strengthen thine heart: wait, I say, on the Lord."

Psalm 27:14

At a certain point in life our patience to wait for the manifestation of a certain thing declines. We feel that we have waited and prayed long enough, that it couldn't possibly take God this long to answer. Remember, you either get desperate like Sarah or give up like Mary and Martha. Let's consider another aspect of waiting in the period of time in which we listen for God's instruction and direction. Sometimes even though we are following God it is a bit tiresome to wait on something with instructions or without sound knowledge as to what we are actually waiting for. The particular passage goes on to say, "be of good courage and He will strengthen thine heart". For instance, our prayers can be centered around God opening doors for a specific business opportunity, but we cannot be prepared for this opportunity literally not having the appropriate paperwork needed and other requirements needed to even qualify. Certain gifts and promotions can become a snare in our lives leading us to places God never intended for us and/or causing us to go backwards instead of forward. There are moments in time in which the enemy capitalizes on a desire in which we have because we value it so much. Even in our efforts to do what is right in the sight of God can be an opportunity for the enemy to get the advantage over us if we are not enlightened. So David said in 1 Chronicles 13:3-4 *"Let us bring the ark of our God back to us, for we did not inquire of[a] it[b] during the reign of Saul.4 The whole assembly agreed to do this, because it seemed right to all the people."* David saw the ark of the covenant and his desire was to restore it to its rightful place. This offer in this moment was too good for him to pass up. After all it was something in which God would surely be pleased with? Ironically, everyone around you can support your decision to accept an offer but it can still not be the offer in which God has for you. David's decision to seize that moment of opportunity cost a life. In life, we take offers based on the ease of access or the fact that everyone around us agrees that is the right way to go. As a result of this we end up in a worse situation. David failed to get instructions regarding the ark of the covenant which in return left him unprepared. So, he went for something which ultimately cost him something more. 2 Samuel 6:7 says 7 *"And the anger of the Lord was kindled against Uzzah; and God smote him there for his error; and there he died by the ark of God."* We can all admit to making similar actions as David did because we were so eager to see a thing happen. And after doing so wondering why things had not turned out as we though they would. No matter what it is that we expect from God or to do for God we must seek His instructions before we take action so that God will order our steps. Often, the wait will involve us moving into the appropriate position in order to receive the manifestation of the courage that comes from hearing His instructions concerning our request and we find strength in carry out those instructions. In light of considering, the wait in this aspect we must then from the onset we must establish the wait as an encouragement to continue to seek Him instead of a moment to wait and see what God will do.

The defining moment when we realize that we could wait is almost always after we experience the consequence of our choice. 8*"And David was displeased, because the Lord had made a breach upon Uzzah: and he called the name of the place Perezuzzah to this day. 9 And David was afraid of the Lord that day, and said, How shall the ark of the Lord come to me? 10 So David would not remove the ark of the Lord unto him into the city of David: but David carried it aside into the house of Obededom the Gittite."* Says 2 Samuel 6:8-10. The displeasure of the choice is not often made know by others and even us when are faced with the decision to accept an offer or not. It is safe to say that if David had known the exact nature of the level of displeasure, he would feel he would probably have made an opposite choice. I am sure that I would probably have reconsidered. However, that's not what typically happens in life. Things usually play out in a very different way. We accept the offer and days and sometimes even weeks later we find ourselves in a bit of a jam, why wait? We wait not because we have nothing more to do or anything of that nature. But we wait to ensure that we have all instructions necessary to receive full benefits of what God had promised. When we do this, we are confident that God has truly spoken to us and it is His desire that we accept what we have been presented. Recall Psalm 27:14 "And He will strengthen thine heart". He makes a solid promise with us that our waiting will not be in vain. The reward after and while waiting is "strength" which is the capacity to wait and be diligent in what He has spoken to us without wavering.

Not only do we find strength in the time of waiting, we also make an altar in our lives which represent God's undeniable power in our life. Jacob made an altar before the Lord at the time in which he was answered by God. Genesis 35:7 *And he built there an altar, and called the place Elbethel: because there God appeared unto him, when he fled from the face of his brother."*

The Bible tells us of many others who became intimate with God in the same way. These are moments in their lives in which they would never forget God. They also lost the human urgency to challenge God in ways in which they had prior to him answering them. They built an altar, remembered God and his mighty acts, then moved on. When we encounter God in such a way that is undeniable, we lose the need to have Him prove Himself to us over and over again in the same manner. Our soul and spirit become completely satisfied that we always put our mind in remembrance of what it is that God has done. In doing so, we are able to trust Him on a greater level each time. After you've been answered build an altar so that you won't forget God. It annoys God when we don't hold dear the things in which He has done. Acting like the children of Israel finding reasons to complain, turning around, and/or wanting to accept the offer of the enemy because we've forgotten to build an altar.

Perhaps at this point in your life you, are wondering why you should wait on a certain thing any longer especially because God has already confirmed it would happen for you. Well waiting causes you to take a moment and reflect on the provisions in which God has already made for you. Let it be the things in which cause you to be persistent and committed to not accept anything less than what God has promised to you. If I can remember who God has been then I will not forget that he is capable of being God without my help.

You Have the Power

In order to receive the promise, you must be in the right position with the right focus. Many of us want the promises of God to come to us in spite of the position we are in. However, it is impossible to receive anything if you are not in the right place. Throughout biblical history we see time and time again that in order for individuals to receive from God there was a specific place they had to be in spiritually, mentally, and physically.

Jesus committing of himself to the will of His father was our victory of triumph over the things of the world. However, He had to go through a process on the night proceeding his crucifixion so that the promise might be fulfilled in the earth. He spent hours in prayer ridding himself of the emotional and mental bondages that were designed to block him from the promise. The scriptures tell us that He prayed until his sweat turned into blood. Therefore, you and I must remain in prayer continuously so that we can be strengthened spiritually until our mind and emotions or no longer in control. We have to yield ourselves unto God until we become what He has called us to be in order to receive exactly what He promised us. If you've ever told God that you trust Him then you're not alone. We've all told Him how much we trust Him with everything that concerns us. It seems that a statement of this sort is often uttered for a period of time without us really experiencing the true reality of the statement. It's not until weeks or sometimes months later when we become faced with the actual reality of trusting God that we find out the length and depth of our trust in Him. Sometimes we allow God's access in some areas while other areas remain off limits. However, at the brink of receiving the promise we must trust God without any borders. This is the time that we must enter in mentally that says we must move forward because that's the only way in which we can receive what He has promised us. Having no borders is very uncomfortable but also rewarding in the same token. There's no one around but you and God which means no one or thing other than God can save you. Once you begin walking you get to a place eventually that you're too far out to go back so you don't turn around but instead raise your head and continue in the direction of God's voice and his presence.

It Is Necessary

Sometimes we want to understand everything- the wrongs, the rights, as well as the in between. It is probably some sort of comfort for us as women or individuals that we will never understand in this lifetime. However, all these things are our choice no matter which way we pose these questions they will be rooted with our choices...The choice to believe or the choice to sit and analyze everything. Jesus said that no one man by taking a thought for his life can add a cubit to his stature. *"which of you by taking thought can add one cubit unto his stature?" (Matthew 6:27)*

26 *"If ye then be not able to do that thing which is least, why take ye thought for the rest?" (Luke 12:26)*

Can you just imagine this? How we spend time thinking and arranging the details of life. If things happen in our favor or not, we still try to figure out how we can keep them under control. There is nothing to think about, whatever God wants you to do he already has the plan. When He wants something from you, He already has a plan. There is no evidence in the bible to solidify that when God requires something from you, he puts you in position to figure it out on your own. Needless to say, the future is history to him already. We must search for the plan that has been written for us. We must release our old plan and the things in which we know how to do or have already experienced before. How do we choose what is needful?

We choose this by going to the least comfortable position ---Least comfortable...Doing the thing that goes against what is common to us. Letting go of what we want and what we have imagined things to be or how it should turn out to be. It is being vulnerable in moments when we really don't have to do so. Meaning it is not a specific mandate of God, but it is the only way to fall completely in alignment with his plan and will for our lives without us compromises or controlling it in any manner. By choosing to believe and just lean on the capacity of God. I must admit that we would feel the most comfortable by being able to analyze things and order them perfect for our lives. We could then wash our hands and say, "all done". However, this will never bring us eternal victory but a sense of personal accomplishment. Jesus encouraged Martha by using her sister Mary as an example he states, "Mary has chosen the one needful thing and it cannot be taken away". Our schedules and life plans can be easily taken away by interruptions forcing us to start over and plan again but choosing to believe and hold on tightly to the master can never be taken away. This connect or arrangement helps to let God take care of us as He promised He would. So, chose that which is the least comfortable, chose that which is needful. Luke 10:42

The Ultimate Offer

This book has discussed the challenges one faces when following God's path for their lives. It is no secret that there are many options available to us as it relates to achievement and success. It is true that the enemies' plans are to get us to compromise and give up on the goals, desires and dreams God has placed within us. As Lamentations 3:35-36 describes it *"To turn aside the right of a man before the face of the most High, 36 To subvert a man in his cause, the Lord approveth not."* In the thick of things, the enemy can present to us offers that are appealing in its nature only to cause us to not fully attain the things in which God has promised us. However, the very clear or vibrant path is necessarily the direction in which God desires for us to go. I have learned that no matter what man or life offers us as a means to help us accomplish things God has given unto us the ultimate offer. First of all, His son who came into earth to show us the way in which we should travel. This ultimate offer will forever stand with great sovereignty because there is nothing that will ever help us in a greater way in reaching success. In addition to this, in following we are aided by the Holy spirit, so that we can fully be what God has intended for us to be.

www.ingramcontent.com/pod-product-compliance
Lightning Source LLC
Chambersburg PA
CBHW061755040426
42447CB00011B/2319